KNOWING THE TRUTH ABOUT

Salvation

John Ankerberg
& John Weldon

HARVEST HOUSE PUBLISHERS
Eugene, Oregon 97402

Scripture quotations marked NIV are from the Holy Bible, New International Version ®, Copyright © 1973, 1978, 1984 by the International Bible Society. Used by permission of Zondervan Publishing House. All rights reserved. The "NIV" and "New International Version" trademarks are registered in the United States Patent and Trademark Office by International Bible Society. Trademark used by permission of International Bible Society.

Verses marked NASB are taken from the New American Standard Bible, © 1960, 1962, 1963, 1968, 1971, 1972, 1973, 1975, 1977 by The Lockman Foundation. Used by permission.

Cover design by Terry Dugan Design, Minneapolis, Minnesota

Other books by
John Ankerberg & John Weldon

The Facts on Abortion	*The Facts on the Mind Sciences*
The Facts on Angels	*The Facts on the Mormon Church*
The Facts on Astrology	*The Facts on Near-Death Experiences*
The Facts on Creation vs. Evolution	*The Facts on the New Age Movement*
The Facts on the Faith Movement	*The Facts on the Occult*
The Facts on False Teaching in the Church	*The Facts on Rock Music*
	The Facts on Roman Catholicism
The Facts on Halloween	*The Facts on Self Esteem, Psychology, and the Recovery Movement*
The Facts on Hinduism	
The Facts on Holistic Health and the New Medicine	*The Facts on Spirit Guides*
	The Facts on UFO's and Other Supernatural Phenomena
The Facts on Homosexuality	
The Facts on Islam	*Knowing the Truth About Jesus The Messiah*
The Facts on the Jehovah's Witnesses	*Knowing the Truth About The Resurrection*
The Facts on Jesus the Messiah	
The Facts on the King James Only Debate	*Knowing the Truth About Salvation*
The Facts on Life After Death	*Knowing the Truth About The Trinity*
The Facts on the Masonic Lodge	

KNOWING THE TRUTH ABOUT SALVATION

Copyright © 1997 by The John Ankerberg Show
Published by Harvest House Publishers
Eugene, Oregon 97402

ISBN 1-56507-539-0

All rights reserved. No portion of this book may be reproduced in any form without the written permission of the Publisher.

Printed in the United States of America.

97 98 99 00 01 02 / LP / 10 9 8 7 6 5 4 3 2

Contents

Everyone shall consider the main end of his life and studies, to know God and Jesus Christ which is eternal life (John 17:3).

—Harvard University's First
College Laws, (1646), p.41[1]

Our repugnance to death increases in proportion to our consciousness of having lived in vain.

—William Hazlett,
The Round Table (1817)

Preface:
Wasted Minds

The mind is too great an asset to waste, for it is the command control of each individual life.

—Ravi Zacharias,
Can Man Live Without God?
(Word, 1994, p. xix)

A poll conducted by the Barna Research Group revealed that 43 percent of born-again Christians agreed with the following statement: "It does not matter what religious faith you follow because all faiths teach similar lessons about life."[2]

If these poll results are valid, they indicate that millions of those claiming to be "born again" agree with most of the rest of the world that Christianity is not unique in the lessons it teaches about life, and that apparently no religion has an absolute claim to religious truth. But no viewpoint could be more wrong.

What these and other poll results really indicate is that a lot of people, both Christians and non-Christians, are uninformed on the subject of comparative religion. Yet critical thinking in this area is vital. (Critical thinking is the reasoning we do in order to determine whether or not a claim is true.) These poll results also betray an unfortunate lack of emphasis on teaching theology, apologetics, and logical thinking at the local church level. The distinguished Christian philosopher Mortimer J. Adler was, unfortunately, correct when he said, "I suspect that most of the individual who have religious faith are content with blind faith. They feel no obligation to understand what they believe. They may even wish not to have their beliefs disturbed by thought. But if the God in whom they believe created them with intellectual and rational powers, that imposes upon them the duty to try to understand the creed of their religion. Not to do so is to verge on superstition."[3]

Of course, religious people are hardly alone in this. Secularists are frequently content with blind faith and just as frequently superstitious. As G.K. Chesterton once observed, "Superstition recurs in all ages, and especially in rationalistic ages. I remember defending the religious tradition against a whole luncheon-table of distinguished agnostics; and before the end of our conversation every one of them had procured from his pocket, or exhibited on his watch-chain, some charm or talisman from which he admitted that he was never separated."[4]

Further, "There is a great deal of research that shows that all people, but especially highly intelligent people, are easily taken in by all kinds of illusions, hallucinations, self-deceptions, and outright bamboozles—all the more so when they have a high investment in the illusion being true."[5]

But if the Bible is clear on anything, it is that we as Christians are responsible to love God with *all* our *minds,* and certainly this involves thinking critically. Indeed, to love God with all our minds is "the greatest commandment" God has given: "Love the Lord your God with all your heart and with all your soul and *with all your mind*. This is the first and *greatest commandment*" (Matthew 22:37,38). This Christian duty includes, at a minimum, a basic knowledge of theology and Christian evidences. Why? Because the Bible teaches that we are to actively defend the faith. How can we do this unless we know the content of the faith (doctrine), how to defend it (apologetics), and how to think clearly and rationally (logical reasoning)? Consider the following Scriptures which speak to each of these concerns: "Dear friends, although I was very eager to write to you about the salvation we share, I felt I had to write and *urge you to contend for the faith* [doctrine] that was once for all entrusted to the saints" (Jude 3; cf., Titus 2:1; 2 Peter 3:18); "But in your hearts set apart Christ as Lord. *Always be prepared to give an answer to everyone who asks you to give the reason for the hope that you have* [apologetics]. But do this with gentleness and respect" (1 Peter 3:15; cf., Philippians 1:7,16); "As his *custom* was, Paul went into the synagogue, and on three Sabbath days he *reasoned* with them from the Scriptures, *explaining and proving* [logical reasoning] that the Christ had to suffer and rise from the dead" (Acts 17:2).

The fact is that the first-century world was a lot like our own. Apart from some pockets of rationalism, mostly in the larger cities, the first-century world was less influenced by western-style modern rationalism than by relativism, subjectivism, and experientialism. In spite of this, Paul said in 2 Corinthians 5:11, "We . . . *persuade* men." Certainly this underscores the importance the Bible places upon the realm of reason and defending the faith.

If God Himself is concerned about logical reasoning and proof, must not His children also be? "'Come now, let us *reason* together,' says the Lord . . ." (Isaiah 1:18); "'He [God] has given *proof* of this [coming judgment] to all men by raising him [Jesus] from the dead'" (Acts 17:31). In light of these and many other Scriptures, every Christian should consider it his or her duty to become informed in Bible doctrine, Christian evidences, and clear thinking.

In light of Adler's comment above, consider the statements of Dr. William Lane Craig, who has earned two Ph.D.'s and is the author of many fine books on Christian evidences. He supplies the following important comments about the implications of Adler's remark, first quoting theologian J. Gresham Machen:

> False ideas are the greatest obstacles to the reception of the gospel. Our churches are filled with Christians who are idling in intellectual neutral. As Christians, their minds are going to waste. One result of this is an immature, superficial faith . . . . Intellectual impoverishment with respect to one's faith can thus lead to spiritual impoverishment as well. But the results of being in intellectual neutral extend far beyond one's self. If Christian laymen don't become intellectually engaged, then we are in serious danger of losing our children. In high school and college Christian teenagers are intellectually assaulted on every hand by a barrage of anti-Christian philosophies and attitudes. As I speak in churches around the country, I continually meet parents whose children have left the faith because there was no one in the church to answer their questions. For the sake of our youth, we desperately need informed parents who are equipped to wrestle with the issues at an intellectual level.

Machen, like Malik, believed that, "The chief obstacle to the Christian religion today lies in the sphere of the intellect," and that it is in that sphere that the issues must be addressed. "The Church is perishing today through the lack of thinking, not through an excess of it."[6]

Are there Christian parents anywhere today who do not care deeply about the spiritual welfare of their own children? Then why does the current situation exist? In part, it is because our culture, with its pluralism, subjectivism, and relativism, finds it easy to replace truth with certainty. And this attitude has influenced the church. But truth is not the same thing as certainty. The people in the above poll may have been certain of their beliefs, but this does not make those beliefs *true*.

Truth is something that is in accordance with fact; certainty refers to a person having no doubt or being fully convinced about something. If we examine the overall religious and philosophical landscape, we find that most people are certain about things that are not true and can rationally be proven false. Philosophers may be certain of their existentialism, relativism, secular humanism, or atheism. Members of religious cults, such as Mormons, Jehovah's Witnesses, Scientologists, and followers of Eastern gurus are certain they are on the right spiritual path. Practitioners of New Age medicine are certain that iridology, homeopathy, and reflexology really work. Astrologers are certain that astrology can reveal personality traits and accurately predict the future. Most scientists are certain of the logically impossible theory of evolution,[7] and mainstream theologians are certain of the so-called "findings" of higher criticism and that the Bible is not inerrant. And on it goes.

Certainty does not prove that the above beliefs are true— only evidence does, and in each case such evidence is sorely lacking. It's the same for traditional world religions such as Roman Catholicism, Islam, Hinduism, Buddhism, Jainism, Sikhism, Confucianism, Sufism, and more recent religions like the Baha'i faith. The committed followers of these religions are all certain about their beliefs. But, obviously, this certainty does not prove their basic beliefs true, because all these religions conflict with one another and no real evidence supports any of these religions.[8] We will logically demonstrate this in a future encyclopedia. (See note 67.)

So, even if 100 percent of all "born-again" Christians were certain that "it does not matter what religious faith you follow," that wouldn't make it true. The issue is whether or not *real* evidence supports the claims of any particular religion and whether it is possible to find absolute truth exclusively in one religion. Is one religion fully true? Are all religions false? Or does it really matter? One could assume that if there is only one true God, there would be only one true religion. The purpose of this booklet is to see if that is so.

Since the dawn of time, human beings have been incurably religious, asking such questions as Who am I? Why am I here? Where did I come from? What happens when I die? How can I know the truth? These are unavoidably *religious* questions and underscore the fact that human history is the history of religion—mankind's attempt to find satisfying answers to these questions.

Although the vast majority of people throughout history have believed in some concept of God, the advent of materialistic theories such as Darwin's theory of evolution and Marx's theory of communism has caused skeptics to add another basic question—Is there a God? If so, how do we know? And who or what is he?[9] The classical and recent proofs of God's existence are beyond the scope of this book; however, in light of them we can know with certainty that the psalmist was correct when he said, "The fool says in his heart, 'There is no God'" (Psalm 14:1). As Sir Isaac Newton, one of the greatest scientists, observed, "He must be blind who from the most wise and excellent contrivances of things cannot see the Infinite Wisdom and Goodness of their Almighty Creator, and he must be mad and senseless who refuses to acknowledge them."[10]

Part I

Introduction:
The God Who Is There

1. What surprising results do we find when we ask non-Christians about God?

In the world today there are only a dozen major religions. But there are literally thousands of minor religions—and thousands of different gods. The Westminster Confession of Faith declares that the chief end of man is to glorify God and to enjoy Him forever. At the time it was written, few Westerners had any real doubts as to which God it referred to. Today it is a different story entirely. The sheer number of religions confuses people when it comes to truth claims. So is it possible to discover which concept of God is true and which religion is true? We think it is. Let's begin by finding out what we can know at the intuitive level.

There is a particular fact that no one, not even the most diehard atheist, can logically deny. The vast majority of men and women throughout history have believed in God. It is probably also true that the majority of the greatest thinkers among humanity, including scientists, have believed in God.[11] In light of this, one might argue atheism is little more than an infected blemish on the face of history.*

If many of the *greatest* intellects of history have believed in God, then it seems a bit presumptuous for anyone to claim absolute assurance there is no God.[12] While this does not prove the Christian view of God, it does say a great deal about *all* skeptical views that characteristically reject theism and supernaturalism.

In *God And*, a disillusioned Catholic priest—Terrance A. Sweeney, president of Jesuit Media Associates in Los Angeles—set out to try and recover his faith. He interviewed 30 famous people and asked each of them three questions: "Who is God to you?"; "Who are you to God?"; and "How has your relationship changed?"[13]

This book illustrates the truth that virtually everybody believes in God at some level, regardless of what they may claim. The famous psychologist Carl Jung once observed that the "idea of an all-powerful divine being is present everywhere, if not consciously recognized, then unconsciously accepted. Therefore I consider it wiser to recognize the idea of God consciously; otherwise something else becomes god, as a rule something quite inappropriate and stupid."[14]

Even if skeptics and others say that they aren't certain of God's existence or that they disbelieve in God, they still know He exists. One reason the Bible spends no time arguing for God's existence is because it really isn't necessary. In the material below we have provided sufficient examples from Sweeney's book to illustrate our point. Collectively, they show the raw power of the intuitive knowledge of God, even when such knowledge is perverted into mysticism and pantheism.

---

*Given the harmful consequences of nontheism historically, documented in texts like Ravi Zacharias' *Can Man Live Without God?*, atheism and similar views are not just blemishes on the face of history but cancers within its body.

Famous writer Kurt Vonnegut, Jr., who describes himself as a rationalist, still believes in God. Even though he judges God's performance as "quite heartless," declaring we have "a lousy God," he nevertheless says that he believes in "pretty much the Unitarian God, where spring is celebrated and where there is a feeling of something terribly important going on in the universe, something unified, an awareness of that" (pp. 86-87). Actor Richard Chamberlain, known for his roles in "Shogun" and "The Thornbirds," declares, "We are pieces of God" (p. 200). Star Trek producer Gene Roddenberry has said, "As nearly as I can concentrate on the question today, I believe I am God; certainly you are; I think we intelligent beings on this planet are all a piece of God, are becoming God" (p. 11). Actor Martin Sheen replies, in response to whether or not he prays, "Only when I get in trouble." Asked where he directs the prayer he says, "It just goes. I feel like I'm making contact. I don't feel that I'm talking to myself when I pray. I don't think people who pray do, do they? If they're really praying, they are in touch with Another, which I think is God, or part of God, or at least the presence of God in us" (p. 23).

Noted movie director Frank Capra makes the following astute observation: "As I got into the creative business, then I realized that creativity and God were connected, directly connected. Whether you believe in God or not. You had to believe, if you believed in creativity, you had to believe in some creator. And if you believed in some creator, where do you end up? You must go to that prime creator, which has set our universe in motion. Things are too ordered in the universe to be the result of chaos. There is no way you can get away from the fact that there's got to be some sort of divine idea to the whole thing" (p. 34).

Even novelist and screenplay writer of *Exorcist* fame, William Peter Blatty, speaks of his relationship with God in quite personal terms: "It's very mysterious that one man, being of sound mind, can give his life for another. I think that kind of love, that kind of inherent goodness speaks very loudly for a good God. And so with all the problems, I personally have always felt that my relationship to God is that of a son who writes lots of letters. He never gets a letter back, but he keeps hearing reports from mutual friends of what his father is doing. And his father seems to be taking the attitude of 'look, trust me, I'm taking care of you.' And I do trust him, I trust God very definitely. There have been so many personal interventions in my life" (p. 45).

Frank Sullivan, Emeritus Professor and Thomas Moore Scholar at Loyola Marymount University, states what most people already know: "To me, proving the existence of God is not important because everybody believes in God no matter what they say. . . . When you look back over your life, carefully, you remember all kinds of moments when you felt God near you; when you felt that somehow or other you lucked out; when you got something you didn't deserve" (pp. 126-27).

William Shoemaker, one of the greatest jockeys in the history of racing, confessed: "I must admit that I'm really not very religious. I do believe in God, but I don't really follow it as well as I probably should. I'm not into it like some people, but I believe in God and sometimes in my life I have asked him to help me when I thought I really needed it. That 's happened to me many times, and I think he's helped me. I think he's been great to me. God's been good to me in my career. I feel like he's trying to look out for me, you know, maybe more so than the average guy" (p. 150).

In an interview, former President George Bush recalled being shot down over the Pacific during World War II. "I was a 20-year-old kid; the other two men in the plane were dead, and flames all over us. Of course, I cried out to God to save me. I remember floating in that rubber raft in the middle of the ocean and yet . . . feeling that God was going to help somehow and that I was going to live."[15]

That God is good to all men is indeed the scriptural testimony. God desires that none should perish and that men should "love life and see good days" (1 Peter 3:10). God "gives to all men generously and without reproach" (James 1:5). In all past generations, God "did good [to you] and gave you rains from heaven and fruitful seasons, satisfying your hearts with food and gladness" (Acts 14:17 NASB). "I know that there is nothing better for men than to be happy and to do good while they live. That everyone may eat and drink, and find satisfaction in all his toil—this is the gift of God" (Ecclesiastes 3:12,13). Truly, "the earth is full of the goodness of the Lord" (Psalm 33:5 KJV). "The Lord is gracious and compassionate, slow to anger and rich in love. The Lord is good to all; he has compassion on all he has made. . . . The Lord is faithful to all his promises and loving toward all he has made. The Lord upholds all those who fall and lifts up all who are bowed down. . . . You open your hand and satisfy the desires of every living thing" (Psalm 145:8,9,13,14,16).

Of course, while God is good and loving, this is not necessarily true of men, and it is certainly not true of the devil and his demons. These are the source of most evil and suffering in the world.[16]

But in spite of the evil in the world, as Ralph Waldo Emerson once noted, "All I have seen teaches me to trust the Creator for all I have not seen." The testimony of everything in life and creation is a testimony to the existence of God, and to His power, majesty, and glory. Walt Whitman commented, "To me every hour of the light and dark is a miracle. Every cubic inch of space is a miracle."[17] Biologist Lewis Thomas once wrote about the fertilized egg: "The mere existence of that cell should be one of the greatest astonishments of the earth. People ought to be walking around all day, all through their waking hours, calling to each other in endless wonderment, talking of nothing except that cell. If anyone does succeed in explaining it, within my lifetime, I will charter a skywriting airplane, maybe a whole fleet of them and send them aloft to write one great exclamation point after another, around the whole sky, until all my money runs out."[18]

Dr. Thomas is quite correct. The ovum is indeed a miracle. And if the DNA content of the human body were printed as chemical "letters," and placed in a book, it would fill the Grand Canyon 50 times! But what about a single atom? A solitary atom—so small that 10,000 of them could be placed one on top of the other in the thickness of this piece of paper—has enough power in it to produce an atomic bomb! Nothing unusual here, either. The truth is there are literally thousands of "miracles" everywhere we look—and yet skeptics tell us confidently, "there is no God."

This sense of wonder and the miraculous, in even ordinary things, also underscores that the intuitive knowledge of God is everywhere. Personal statements such as those cited above are repeated in various ways throughout Sweeney's book—and could, certainly, be repeated six billion more times were we to interview everyone in the world. They clearly illustrate the truth of Romans 1 and 2 which declare that everyone intuitively *knows* God exists, everyone has a conscience, and everyone knows they are personally accountable to a divine Being. For example, the following Chinese belief in divine accountability is seen in every religion and culture in one manner or another: "A very old idea in Chinese philosophy holds that there are spirits, in both microcosm and macrocosm, that record one's good and bad deeds."[19] Because the sense of responsibility to a higher power exists universally, at some level and in some way all men expect a future judgment. That is one reason the fear of death is also universal: "All their lives [men are] held in slavery by their fear of death" (Hebrews 2:15).

Regardless, as far as we know, none of the statements in Sweeney's book or by the others were, at that time, made by genuine Christians. When non-Christians, secular or religious, make statements about God that have varying degrees of truth in them, this certainly says something about what people know intuitively. But an interesting point is that even though people know that God has been good to them, they usually ignore Him. They know God exists (Romans 1:20), they "believe" in God, they realize God has been good to them—and yet they live their lives as if God *doesn't* exist! Their "belief" in God is intuitive and self-serving, not genuine and biblical. As the esteemed philosopher Mortimer Adler recalled, prior to his own conversion to Christianity, "I simply did not *wish* to exercise a will to believe."[20] Famous novelist Aldous Huxley wrote frankly that, "Most ignorance is vincible ignorance. We don't know because we don't *want* to know. It is our will that decides how and upon which subjects we shall use our intelligence."[21,22]

Have you ever wondered why so many people speak in terms of being *blessed*, of being *given* gifts, etc., when they don't believe in God? They accept the gifts, but it seems they rarely acknowledge God as the Giver. In a TV news report of an earlier interview (given on the day he died) October 10, 1985, Yul Brynner noted, "I've been blessed with this special gift. Who could ask for more in life?" In a *20/20* interview October 10, 1985, rock musician Bob Dylan commented, "I don't have any faith in myself that I can do anything. I just pull it off. I'm amazed I can even do it." The sense or intuitive perception that there is something good going on and something more involved than the life we know has been a constant theme in human discourse and activities throughout history. To cite a modern example, Sir John Eccles is one of the foremost brain scientists of this century, and was awarded the Nobel prize for medicine. He and his co-author write the following concerning the personal conclusions they draw from natural theology:

> We think science has gone too far in breaking down man's belief in his spiritual greatness and has given him the belief that he is merely an insignificant animal that has arisen by chance and necessity in an insignificant planet lost in the great cosmic immensity. The principal trouble with mankind today is that the intellectual leaders are too arrogant in their self-sufficiency.

We must realize the great unknowns in the material makeup and operation of our brains, and the relationship of brain to mind, in our creative imagination and in the uniqueness of the psyche. *When we think of these unknowns as well as the unknown of how we come to be in the first place, we should be much more humble.* Mankind would be cured of its alienation if that message [of man's spiritual significance] could be expressed with all the authority of scientists and philosophers as well as with the imaginative insights of artists. We pray that man may develop a transforming faith in the meaning and significance of this wonderful, even unbelievable, adventure given to each of us on this lovely and salubrious earth of ours . . . In the context of natural theology we come to the belief that we are creatures with some supernatural meaning that is as yet ill defined. We cannot think more than that we are all part of some great design. Each of us can have the belief of acting in some unimaginable supernatural drama. We should give all we can in order to play our part in this life on earth.[23]

If anything may be concluded from the study of man, or human history, or life generally, it is that everyone intuitively *knows* that God exists, even the most brilliant among us. However, some readers may be thinking at this point that we really haven't been fair to the convictions of atheists and other skeptics. After all, such people can sound very convincing when they claim they have *never* believed in God and are *absolutely* certain no God exists.

2. Is there an innate knowledge of God in atheists, skeptics, and other opponents of Christianity?

The truth is that even those whose personal philosophies have been intensely opposed to the Christian faith can't escape God. Noted skeptical philosopher Bertrand Russell, the author of *Why I Am Not a Christian and Other Essays*, once wrote in a letter, "The centre of me is always and eternally a terrible pain—a curious wild pain—a searching for something beyond what the world contains, something transfigured and infinite."[24] The occult psychologist Carl Jung, whose damage inflicted on Christianity is hard to calculate, wrote in his autobiography, *Memories, Dreams, Reflections*, "I find that all my thoughts circle around God like the planets around the sun, and are as irresistibly attracted by Him. I would feel it to be the grossest sin if I were to oppose any resistance to this force."[25] This is the same man who, grimly, said more than once, "They would have burned me as a heretic in the middle ages."[26] Werner Erhard, whose est/The Forum seminars are subtly yet profoundly anti-Christian, recalls an experience with God concerning the sins he had committed against his family. In an apartment with a large window overlooking the ocean he recalls, "As I sat there I had a conversation with God. It was a holy experience; it had not the circumstances but the experience of holiness about it. I was literally forced to rise from my chair, and then forced to my knees. And I prayed for forgiveness."[27]

Atheists, again, are certain there isn't a God. One Buddhist makes a statement common in our culture, "We are not in God's hands; we are in our own."[28] But such convictions are really quite unwise since no atheist could exist for even a second longer apart from the preserving hand of God. Indeed, our moment-by-moment existence depends solely upon His goodness and upholding power, for He is "sustaining all things by his powerful word" (Hebrews 1:3) and "in him all things hold together" (Colossians 1:17). As the prophet Daniel told the pagan King Belshazzar, "[Y]ou have exalted yourself against the Lord of heaven ... But the God in whose hand are your life-breath and your ways, you have not glorified" (Daniel 5:23 NASB).

The simple fact is that atheist beliefs do not square with human perceptions. In *The Tao of Psychology*, Zen practitioner Jean Bolen, M.D., observes that we all, in some ways, "feel ourselves part of a divine, dynamic, interrelated universe."[29] "Whether I am lying under the stars or sitting in Zazen meditating, or at peace in prayer, the *intuitive* knowledge that there is a patterned universe, or an underlying *meaning* to all experience, or a primal source, *to which I am connected*, always evokes a feeling of reverence. It is something *known* rather than thought about, so that explanatory words are inadequate."[30]

She also recalls, "I went to the mountains when I was a youngster and lay in my sleeping bag under the stars, seeing the vastness of the Milky Way above. What my eyes saw, my soul experienced. I felt a sense of reverence and awe at the boundlessness and beauty of the universe. It touched me. I felt God's presence in the mountains, trees and immense sky."[31]

As an editorial in *Reader's Digest* commented, "Walk out on a balmy August night, when meteors have streaking tracks overhead, and the belief will come unbidden that all of that splendor must reflect a reigning intelligence, that such intelligence will give evidence of its existence . . ."[32]

In the daytime, we cannot see the stars, but we know they exist—we see them at night. Someone who lives at the north pole, where light shines 24 hours a day and it is never night, might not believe there are stars because he has never seen them. Still, they would exist—as massive, awesome realities. Because we cannot yet see something (God), does not mean it (He) does not exist. At the final judgment, no one will doubt God's existence in the slightest.

The Bible is also clear that all men know of God and that all men are "close" to God. In reference to the incarnation of Jesus Christ it says, "The true light that gives light to *every man* was coming into the world" (John 1:9). In Romans 1 we read:

> The wrath of God is being revealed from heaven against all the godlessness and wickedness of men who suppress the truth by their wickedness, since *what may be known about God is plain* to them, because God *has made it plain* to them. For since the creation of the world God's invisible qualities—his eternal power and divine nature—have been *clearly seen*, being *understood* from what has been made, so that men are without excuse. For although they knew God, they neither glorified him as God nor gave thanks to him, but their thinking became futile and their foolish hearts were darkened (Romans 1:18-21).

The term "since the creation of the world" includes all men and women who have ever lived. So Romans 1 must also be true for all atheists and skeptics. God doesn't say He has placed a knowledge of Himself in everyone except atheists and skeptics. To illustrate, even the most famous atheist of the twentieth century, Jean-Paul Sartre, confessed the following in an interview just before his death, published in *Harper's* magazine for February, 1984: "Even if one does not believe in God, there are elements of the idea of God that remain in us."[33] Sartre goes on to state, even though he had supposedly been a convinced atheist from the age of eight or nine, that the structure of consciousness[34] and his own intuitive awareness and experience in life almost compelled him to accept the existence of God: "As for me, I don't see myself as so much dust that has appeared in the world but as a being that was expected, prefigured, called forth. In short, as a being that could, it seems, come only from a creator; and this idea of a creating hand that created me refers me back to God. Naturally this is not a clear, exact idea that I set in motion every time I think of myself. It contradicts many of my other ideas; but it is there, floating vaguely. And when I think of myself I *often* think rather in this way, for wont of *being able to think otherwise.*"[35]

Even as a leading atheist, Sartre could never escape God because he had not only been *created*, he had been created "in God's image" (Genesis 1:26,27). God had placed the knowledge of Himself directly into the being of Sartre. So, even though Sartre further stated, "This life owes nothing to God," he actually knew that his atheism was a personal choice to ignore God, not proof that God didn't exist.

And whether or not a person admits it, virtually everyone, atheists and skeptics included, at some point in life, searches *for* God or for something beyond themselves that will give meaning to life. Again, Sartre himself confessed, "God is silent and that I cannot deny; everything in myself calls for God and that I cannot forget."[36] Thus, "in his philosophical writings, in his biographies, and in his plays, Sartre is definitely concerned with man's relationship to God and to the realm of the holy."[37]

Sartre thought God was "silent," but of course, God isn't silent at all. The learned Apostle Paul told the Epicurean and Stoic philosophers at the Areopagus in Athens, Greece:

> [God] "himself gives all men life and breath and everything else. From one man he made every nation of men, that they should inhabit the whole earth; and he determined the times set for them and the exact places where they should live. God did this so that men would seek him and perhaps reach out for him and find him, though he is not far from each one of us. For in him we live and move and have our being. As some of your own poets have said, 'We are his offspring.'" (Acts 17:25-28).

If everyone is the offspring of God, if God is not far from us, if we have our being in Him, if everyone is made in His image, and if God has "enlightened," "clearly revealed," and "made Himself known" to every person who ever lived, then God has hardly been "silent," even apart from His personal revelation in the Bible. What this means is that a lot of skeptics know more than they're saying.

In *Eternity in Their Hearts*, Don Richardson provides many examples showing how the concept of one true supreme God has existed throughout history in hundreds of cultures around the world. For example, concerning the "Sky-god" among folk religionists he writes:

> In hundreds of instances attested to by literally millions of folk religionists worldwide, the Sky-god does exactly what El Elyon [the biblical God] did through Melchizedek [to Abraham, in Genesis 14]. He cheerfully acknowledges the approaching messengers of Yahweh as *His* messengers! He takes pains to make it very clear—He Himself is none other than the very God those particular foreigners proclaim! This is surely a powerful extra-biblical evidence for the authenticity of the Bible as revelation from the one true and universal God! It is also, as we shall see later, the prime reason on the human level for the phenomenal acceptance Christianity has found among people of so many folk religions on this planet. In addition, Scripture after Scripture has testified down through the centuries that our God has not left Himself without witness—even apart from the preaching of the gospel (see Acts 14:16,17). That witness—though different in kind and quality from the biblical witness itself is still a witness to Him! . . . If you belong to a tradition which has been teaching Christians for centuries that the rest of the world sits in total darkness and knows zilch about God, it becomes a little embarrassing to have to say, "We have been wrong. In actual fact, more than 90 percent of this world's folk religions acknowledge at least the existence of God. Some even anticipate His redeeming concern for mankind."

> The Apostle John's statement that the world lies in spiritual wickedness (see 1 John 5:19) needs to be coupled with the Apostle Paul's acknowledgment that God has not left Himself without witness. For that witness has penetrated the wickedness to some degree almost everywhere!

> As the Apostle John put it, "The light shines in the darkness, but the darkness has not overpowered it" (John 1:5, footnote). John further specified the "light" he describes is the "true light that gives light to every man" (1:9).[38]

If all this is true, then *everyone* does know there is a God and they also know certain things about Him. Since God

Himself has been their teacher, there is no possibility of failure. There are no atheists finally, in foxholes, crashing airplanes, surgery rooms, or anywhere else.

Indeed, to suppress the truth that God has placed within each man only leads to varying degrees of neurosis. As the noted psychologist Rollo May wrote in *The Art of Counseling*, "I have been startled by the fact that practically every genuine atheist with whom I have dealt has exhibited unmistakable neurotic tendencies. How [do we] account for this curious fact?"[39] And, perhaps even more telling, according to Senior Pastor Jess Moody of the First Baptist Church of Van Nuys, California, "Lie detector tests were administered to more than 25,000 people. One of the questions was, 'Do you believe in God?' In every case, when a person answered no, the lie detector said he was lying."[40]

Man's biggest folly is to ignore the God who is there (the God we all know is there), and to live our life as if He were irrelevant. It is folly because it is a kind of intuitive and intellectual madness, not to mention potentially dangerous. It's like a man in a boat in the middle of the ocean saying, "there are no sharks" when he sees fins all around him. Because he is lost at sea, he has radioed for help and he sees a rescue boat on the horizon. His salvation is only a few hours away and yet he decides to go swimming.

Terrance Sweeney concluded his book with the following comment, "The overwhelming conclusion from the sum of the interviews is that God, or the One people refer to as God, is very much a part of human experience and consciousness."[41] So, everyone believes in God. But if God exists and if there is only one true God, then how do we find Him?

Part II

Analysis: The Truth That Is There: Can a Person Find the One True God?

Truth is Christianity's most enduring asset.

— Carl F. Henry,
Carl Henry at His Best
(Multnomah, 1989, p. 203)

It is our conviction that, considered historically, probably millions of people have done just this: they have found the one true God and come to know Him personally. Even today probably several hundreds of millions of people worldwide could truthfully make the same claim. The only issue is, does the evidence support the possibility of knowing the one true God?

In order to begin to answer such a question, controversial as it is to a pluralistic or secular mind-set as ours, sometimes it is easier to reduce things to their basic concepts. This will help us see how unique Christianity really is.

3. What happens when we compare the basics of Christianity to other philosophies and religions?

One way to illustrate the uniqueness of Christianity is to examine theological concepts. At the time of the patriarch Abraham, the entire world was mired in polytheism. So—in a world of endless gods, how did a belief in one God ever originate? This is a more profound question than it seems because, apart from the Christian explanation, everyone agrees this is a mystery. But if we assume divine revelation— that the one true God had revealed Himself to Abraham— there is a satisfactory explanation. Again, at this time no other religion in the world, no other culture in the world, was monotheistic. Here is the utter uniqueness of Christian beginnings: Judaism *was* monotheistic.

In fact, we can examine theological concepts in many different ways and all point to the uniqueness of Christianity. For example, among the dozen major categories of Christian theology, almost all of which are unique, is the doctrine of soteriology or salvation.*

If we break down the doctrine of salvation into its component parts (see Bottom Note), we discover teachings that are found nowhere else in the world. How do we account for one religion that is unique theologically—not to mention

---

* Basic Christian doctrines include Bibliology, the doctrine of the Bible; Theology Proper, the doctrine of God (theism, Trinitarianism); Angelology, the doctrine of angels, elect and reprobate; Anthropology, the doctrine of man; Harmartiology, the doctrine of sin; Ecclesiology, the doctrine of the church; Christology, the doctrine of Christ; Pneumatology, the doctrine of the Holy Spirit; and Eschatology, the doctrine of last things. All these doctrines are unique in key ways when compared with those in other religions. Under the doctrine of salvation, we find the doctrines of depravity, imputation, grace, propitiation/atonement, reconciliation, calling, regeneration, union with Christ, conversion (repentance/faith), justification, adoption, sanctification, eternal security (perseverance), election/predestination, redemption, and death, resurrection and the final state. Despite the surface similarities of some of these doctrines to those in other faiths, these doctrines are also unique.

philosophically and experientially—when all the other religions of the world teach nothing new? The common themes of other religions include salvation by works, polytheism and occultism. Even Islam's monotheism was not unique. So how do we account for the development of completely unique teachings such as monotheism, the Trinity, salvation by grace, the doctrine of depravity, resurrection to personal bodily immortality, and a score of others, when they are still a mystery? In other words, there never existed any impetus for their initial development. So again, how do we explain them apart from divine revelation? The fact is, we don't.

To illustrate, consider just the doctrine of grace. Martin Luther, the great church reformer, was right when he said that there were really only two religions in the world, the religion of works and the religion of grace. If we were to examine all the different religions that exist today and then go back through history and examine all religions that have ever existed, we would find that there is no exception. All other religions teach salvation by meritorious works. Christianity is the only religion that teaches salvation solely by grace through faith alone. This simple fact makes it stand entirely apart from other religions. It also necessitates an answer to the question, "Why, out of the thousands of religions throughout history, is there only *one* that teaches salvation by grace?" How do we logically explain the origin of only one religion that teaches something no other religion ever has when there was *never* any human basis for such a belief to arise? In other words, how did mankind ever *acquire* a religion of pure grace with salvation as a *free* gift when the natural bent of the human heart is one of self-justifying works and earning one's own salvation? Why does one religion stand out like a floodlight among a group of candles?

The most reasonable (and only satisfactory) answer is divine revelation. This is exactly what the Bible claims. "I want you to know, brothers, that the gospel I preached is not something that man made up. I did not receive it from any man, nor was I taught it; rather, I received it *by revelation* from Jesus Christ" (Galatians 1:11,12). Thus, the gospel of Christianity is not something man made up because man never would have made it up; it goes against the grain of self-justification too sharply. The one true God personally revealed the one true way of salvation in the Bible. Obviously, He didn't reveal it in the scriptures of other religions since they contradict the Bible's most basic teachings, and God does not contradict Himself nor is He a God of confusion (Titus 1:2; 1 Corinthians 14:33).

In essence, observers of religion and critics of Christianity must explain why there *is* one religion of grace amidst universal religions of works. It can only be because the one true God who exists is a God of grace (Ephesians 1:7; 2:8) that we find a single religion of grace among all that oppose it.

A related approach would be to evaluate different concepts of origins. In philosophical apologetics this approach is taken by the late Christian philosopher Dr. Francis Schaeffer in *He Is There and He Is Not Silent*.

How do we attempt to explain our existence? In terms of concepts of origins or explanations of reality, though there are hundreds of religions and philosophies, when reduced to their most common elements, there are only a relatively few options:

1. The finite personal—creation by the gods.
2. The infinite personal—creation by a God such as the Muslim Allah.
3. The infinite impersonal monistic—creation (self-emanation) by the Brahman of Hinduism.
4. The materialistic impersonal—e.g., creation by chance, i.e., the theory of evolution. (Matter is eternal; the "big bang," etc.)
5. The infinite personal Triune—creation by the God of the Bible.

Dr. Schaeffer's argument is essentially this: Only by beginning with the Christian view of origins can one adequately explain the universe as we know it in terms of metaphysics, epistemology, and morality. (Metaphysics deals with the nature of existence, truth, and knowledge; epistemology with how we know; and morality with how we should live.)

The problem with options one through four is that they cannot adequately explain and/or logically support these key philosophical doctrines. For example, in option one, the finite personal origin, the mythical and bickering, capricious and copulating finite gods (whether of the ancient Greeks and Romans or the modern Hindus and Buddhists) can't explain the nature of existence because they aren't big enough to create the world, let alone provide us with the infinite reference point we need in order to have an absolute truth or to justify meaning in life. The preeminent atheist philosopher we discussed earlier, Jean Paul Sartre, was correct in stating that man required an infinite reference point in order for life to have any meaning. Since Sartre didn't believe there was such a reference point, he stated, "Man is absurd, but he must grimly act as if he were not"[42] and "Man is a useless passion."[43] On the other hand, the infinite personal triune God of the Bible is big enough to create the universe and big enough to provide man with an infinite reference point to give his existence meaning. Nor can amoral gods provide any logical basis for moral living. But the God of the Bible, who is infinitely righteous, holy, and immutable can provide such a basis.

The problem with option two, the infinite personal origin, is that such a God seems ultimately dependent upon his creation in order to express the attributes of his own nature and personality. In other words, for all eternity prior to creation this God would have been alone with himself. With whom does He communicate? Whom does He love? (In part, this may explain why the absolute transcendence and "otherness" of the distant Muslim deity, Allah, is stressed so heavily in Islam and why Allah is not truly a God of love.) It would appear that such a God is "forced" to create and is subsequently *dependent* upon his creation for expressing the attributes of his own personality—and is, therefore, not a *truly* independent or free divine Being. The concept of a God who is dependent on something else is hardly an adequate concept of God. The Christian view of origins solves this problem because the triune God as Father, Son, and Holy Spirit had no need to create in order to express His attributes of personality. The members of the Godhead communicated together, loved one another, etc., for all eternity and are never dependent upon their creation for anything.

The problem with option three, the infinite, impersonal, monistic origin, is that it portrays a God who is infinite but impersonal and therefore it gives no basis for explaining the origin of personality or any logical reason for personhood to have absolute meaning. This explains why, in both Hinduism and Buddhism, the personality is seen as an "enemy" and is finally destroyed by absorption into Brahman or Nirvana. Not only the material creation but human existence, body and personality, are either an illusion, as in Hinduism (*maya*) or so empty and impermanent, as in Buddhism (*sunyata*), that they are ultimately meaningless. In the end, man is a hindrance to spiritual enlightenment and must be "destroyed" to find "liberation." As Dr. Frits Staal comments in "Indian Concepts of the Body," "Whatever the alleged differences between Hindu and Buddhist doctrines, one conclusion follows from the preceding analysis. No features of the individual personality survive death in either state."[44] But is an impersonal "immortality" truly meaningful when it extinguishes our existence forever? Is it even desirable? As Ajith Fernando, who has spoken to hundreds of Buddhists and

Hindus, illustrates, "When I asked a girl who converted to Christianity from Buddhism through our ministry what attracted her to Christianity, the first thing she told me was, 'I did not want Nirvana.' The prospect of having all her desires snuffed out after a long and dreary climb was not attractive to her."[45]

Monistic philosophies provide no explanation for the diversity within the creation. If "God is one," then diversity—all creation—is by definition part of the illusion of duality. That includes all moral views, all human hopes and aspirations, and all else that matters. In the end, we are left with a nihilistic outlook despite having an infinite reference point.

The infinite triune God of the Bible addresses this issue as well. Because God *is* personal, human personality has genuine and eternal significance. The only kind of eternity that has any meaning, or gives this life any meaning, is an eternity of *personal* immortality. And because Christianity involves a philosophy of religious dualism, God is the creator of a *real* creation. The creation is not simply the illusory emanation of an impersonal divine substance. As a result, there is no need to face the very destructive consequences of nihilism.

Option number four, the materialistic impersonal origin, has similar problems to option three. Ultimate reality is still impersonal, although not a divine substance. Ultimate reality is dead matter. There is no God, period. Where does anyone find any dignity or meaning when our own self-portrait is the cold atoms of deep space? In the end, after a single, probably difficult, life, we die forever. Although such a fate is infinitely more merciful than the endless reincarnations and final dissolutions of Hinduism and Buddhism, it is still far too nihilistic and despairing for most people to live out practically. As Leslie Paul observed, in this view, "All life is no more than a match struck in the dark and blown out again. The final result is to deprive it completely of meaning."[46]

Famous philosophers and social commentators alike have stated the logical results of the death of God at the hands of materialism. Albert Camus said, "I proclaim that I believe in nothing and that everything is absurd."[47] Andy Warhol declared of his six-hour film showing a man sleeping, "It keeps you from thinking. I wish I were a machine."[48] "Death of God" philosopher Nietzsche informs us that the inhumane aspects of man "are perhaps the fertile soil out of which alone all humanity can grow" and then proceeds to destroy everything by having the Madman give us his famous discourse on God's death:

> The madman sprang into their midst and pierced them with his glances. Then "Whither is God?" he cried. "I shall tell you. *We have killed him*—you and I." All of us are his murderers. But how have we done this? How were we able to drink up the sea? Who gave us the sponge to wipe away the entire horizon? What did we do when we unchained this earth from its sun? Whither is it moving now? Away from all suns? Are we not plunging continually? Backward, sideward, forward, in all directions? Is there any up or down left? Are we not straying through an infinite nothing? Do we not feel the breath of empty space? Has it not become colder? Is not night and more night coming on all the while? Must not lanterns be lit in the morning? Do we not hear anything yet of the noise of the grave-diggers who are burying God? Do we not smell anything yet of God's decomposition? Gods, too, decompose. God is dead, and we have killed him.
>
> How shall we, the murderers of all murderers, comfort ourselves? What was holiest and most powerful of all that the world has yet owned has bled to death under our knives.
>
> Who will wipe this blood off us?. . . Is not the greatness of this deed too great for us? Must not we ourselves become gods simply to seem worthy of it?[49]

Walter Kaufman comments that "Nietzsche prophetically envisages himself as a madman: to have lost God means madness; and when mankind will discover that it has lost God, universal madness will break out."[50]

In essence, the problem with option No. 4 is that it is utterly impossible to rationally explain the origin of life materialistically on evolutionary or any other grounds.[51(cf. R.C. Sproul, *Not a Chance*)]

However, when we begin with the Christian religion—an infinite and personal triune concept of origins—we *logically* and reasonably have an explanation for things as they are— human personality, the desire for meaning in life, the yearning for personal immortality, a real creation having both unity and diversity, a transcendent basis for absolute morality, etc. Indeed, the nature of the creation itself mirrors the nature of its Creator. For example, just as there is unity and diversity in the Godhead—*three* centers of consciousness in *one* divine essence—so there is unity and diversity in the creation. Whether we speak of men, trees, butterflies or snowflakes, every category of life is the "same but different." All men, trees, butterflies or snowflakes are alike but no two are identical. In one sense, God has not only made man, but the creation itself, "after His image."

In conclusion, the fact that Christianity logically and adequately explains more about the facts of our existence than any other religion argues, in part, for biblical Christianity being the true religion. Other reasons are given in questions 6-8.

For the moment, let's assume that the Bible really is the only revelation of God, that biblical Christianity is the one fully true religion and that, as the Bible teaches, Jesus Christ is the only way to God and salvation. In John 14:6, Jesus declared that He was the only way to God *because He* alone was the atoning sacrifice for the world's sin: "the Son of Man did not come to be served, but to serve, and to give his life as a ransom for many" (Matthew 20:28); "This is my blood of the covenant, which is poured out for many for the forgiveness of sins" (Matthew 26:28).

It is a fact that no religion can logically deny the reality of sin and equally a fact that no religion but Christianity solves the problem of sin. To argue that sin is merely an "illusion" or "ignorance," as Hinduism and Buddhism do, does not solve the problem of sin. To argue as Islam does, that God can forgive sin by fiat apart from a just payment to God's justice and holiness, is inconceivable if God is truly infinitely righteous. If, as the Bible teaches, the just penalty for sin is physical and spiritual death, then only Jesus has solved the problem of sin. As a true man Jesus could die for man's sin. As true God He could both pay the required penalty to infinite justice and also resurrect from the dead as proof the penalty had been paid. Thus, when Jesus died on the cross he took in His own person the penalty for our sin. Because He was "made sin," and thus immediately prior to physical death separated from God, Jesus thereby paid the penalty for sin that was due to God's justice, physical and spiritual death. He truly solved the problem of sin, and its consequence, death (Romans 3:23)

Did Buddha die for our sins? Did Mohammed die for our sins? Did Lao Tze, the founder of Taoism? Or Moses? Did Zoroaster, the founder of Parsism? Or Guru Nanak, the founder of Sikhism? None of these men ever claimed to do this. Put another way, isn't it rather startling that not one of

he founders of a religion ever claimed and offered proof that
e solved the problems of human sin, evil, and death, the
nost fundamental human problems of all? Only Jesus solved
he sin problem and conquered death, so logically, only Jesus
s the way of salvation and the way to God and eternal life. J.
. Packer once noted, "No philosophy that will not teach us
ow to master death is worth two pence to us," and L. P.
acks wrote in *The Inner Sentinel*, "No religion is worth its
ame unless it can prove itself more than a match for death."

We reiterate, because Jesus is the *only* incarnation of God,
nd God's *only* begotten Son (John 3:16,18), when He died on
he cross for human sin, and rose from the dead, He became
he only possible way of salvation and eternal life for all men
nd women. This is why the Bible teaches, "Salvation is
und in *no one else*, for there is *no other name under heaven
iven to men by which we must be saved*" (Acts 4:12).
urther, "This is good, and pleases God our Savior, who
ants all men to be saved and to come to a knowledge of the
ruth. For there is one God and *one* mediator between God
nd men, the man Christ Jesus, who gave himself as a
ansom for all men—the testimony given in its proper time"
Timothy 2:3-6). All this is why Jesus Himself warned, "if
ou do not believe that I am the one I claim to be, you will
deed die in your sins" (John 8:24).

But if Jesus really is the only way to God, does this make
e Christian faith "narrow-minded " or "intolerant " as so
any people seem to think? We will answer this question
om the perspectives of comparative religion, common
nse, and historical evidence. When we answer the question,
What about other religions?" we will show that Jesus' utter
niqueness makes His claims of being exclusively the way of
lvation worth considering. In Question 5, we will prove
at exclusivity in salvation is not inconsistent with how we
ve our lives in other areas, noting that most other religions
so claim to be the best or only way. Therefore, it is simply a
atter of the evidence as to which exclusive truth claim, if
y, is true.

What about other religions?

When we consider all the great religious teachers, leaders,
d prophets who have ever lived, who is the equal of Jesus?
ot Moses, Confucius, Buddha, or Lao Tze (Taoism), who
ver claimed to be anything other than sinful men. Not
ohammed, Joseph Smith, Zoroaster, or Guru Nanak
ikhism), who never gave any proof they were true prophets

of God. Not Brahma, Vishnu, Shiva, or Krishna, who were
only mythical deities. Not Mahavira (Jainism) or the
founder/leader of any other religion the world has known
has ever been like Jesus. Neither animism, Buddhism,
Confucianism, Hinduism, Islam, Jainism, Judaism, Mormon-
ism, Shinto, Sikhism, Sufism, Taoism, Zoroastrianism nor any
other religious belief outside Christianity has anything that
can even be slightly compared to Jesus.

Thus, if we examine the specific claims of the founders of
the great religions, we find that none of them claims what
Jesus does. In *The Koran* the Muslim prophet Mohammed
states, "Muhammad is naught but a messenger" and "Surely
I am no more than a human apostle."[52] In fact, several times in
The Koran, Mohammed is acknowledged as sinful, asks for
giveness from God, or is even rebuked by God.[53]

Mohammed confessed he was sinful, but Jesus claimed
He was sinless. Mohammed only claimed to be a prophet of
God; Jesus claimed to be God. Mohammed was rebuked by
God; Jesus never was—in fact, He said, "I always do what
pleases Him" (John 8:29).

Consider Buddha for a more in-depth illustration. The
Buddha simply claimed to be an enlightened man, one who
could show others how to escape the futility of this world and
find eternal release from suffering in a state of individual
nonexistence called "nirvana." After his alleged enlightenment, the Buddha said he realized the importance of
maintaining an attitude of equanimity towards all things
because this attitude helps one to end the cycle of rebirth,
attain permanent release from the human condition and enter
nirvana: "Monks, I'm a Brahmana [enlightened being], one to
ask a favor of, ever clean-handed, wearing my last body. I am
inexorable, bear no love nor hatred toward anyone. I have the
same feelings for respectable people as for the low; or more
persons as for the immoral; for the depraved as for those who
observe the rules of good conduct. You disciples, do no
affirm that the Lord Buddha reflects thus within himself, 'I
bring salvation to every living being.' Subhuti entertain no
such delusive thought! Because in reality there are no living
beings to whom the Lord Buddha can bring salvation."
Houston Smith in *The Religions of Man* comments about the
Buddha, "Notwithstanding his own objectivity toward himself, there was constant pressure during his lifetime to turn
him into a god. He rebuffed all these categorically, insisting
that he was human in every respect. He made no attempt to
conceal his temptations and weaknesses, how difficult it had

been to attain enlightenment, how narrow the margin by which he had won through, how fallible he still remained."[55]

Clive Erricker, a lecturer and prolific writer in the field of religious studies with a special interest in Buddhism, writes accurately of the Buddha when he discussed what Buddha did *not* claim: "Indeed, he did not even claim that his teachings were a unique and original source of wisdom. . . . [Citing John Bowker in *Worlds of Faith*, 1983] Buddha always said, 'Don't take what I'm saying [i.e., on my own authority], just try to analyze as far as possible and see whether what I'm saying makes sense or not. If it doesn't make sense, discard it. If it does make sense, then pick it up.'"[56]

Buddha claimed merely a personal enlightenment designed to escape human nature; Jesus claimed (in His *own* nature) to *be* the light of the world. Buddha claimed it was wrong to consider him one who brings salvation to men because men, having no permanent reality, do not finally exist; Jesus taught that He came to bring salvation to all men and to dignify their existence eternally. Buddha promised to give others enlightenment so that they might find nirvana, a state of personal dissolution in the afterlife; Jesus promised to give men abundant life and eternal personal immortality in heaven. Buddha had the *same* feelings for good and evil; Jesus exalted righteousness and hated evil.

Confucius said, "As to being a Divine Sage or even a Good Man, far be it for me to make any such claim."[57] If Confucius denied that he was divine or even a good man, Jesus claimed He was divine and morally perfect.

Zoroaster claimed to be only a prophet. "I was ordained by Thee at the first. All others I look upon with hatred of spirit."[58] Lao-Tze and Guru Nanak sum up the attitude of all the great religious founders when they confessed their humanity and even their ignorance. For example, Lao-Tze, the founder of Taoism, said, "I alone appear empty. Ignorant am I, O so ignorant! I am dull! I alone am confused, so confused!"[59] Even in the latter part of his life, Guru Nanak, the founder of Sikhism, still struggled to achieve enlightenment and lamented over his own spiritual darkness: "I have become perplexed in my search. In the darkness I find no way. Devoted to pride, I weep in sorrow. How shall deliverance be obtained?"[60]

In *The World's Living Religions*, Robert Hume, Professor of the History of Religions, comments that there are three features of Christian faith that "cannot be paralleled anywhere among the religions of the world."[61] These include the character of God as a loving heavenly Father, the character of the founder of Christianity as the Son of God, and the work of the Holy Spirit. Further, "All of the nine founders of religion, with the exception of Jesus Christ, are reported in their respective sacred scriptures as having passed through a preliminary period of uncertainty, or of searching for religious light. All the founders of the non-Christian religions evinced inconsistencies in their personal character; some of them altered their practical policies under change of circumstances. Jesus Christ alone is reported as having had a consistent God-consciousness, a consistent character himself, and a consistent program for his religion."[62]

Again, Jesus is unique in the claims He makes for Himself. He says, "I am the light of the world. Whoever follows me will never walk in darkness, but will have the light of life" (John 8:12). How many other men have ever said that? Jesus said, "I am the way and the truth and the life. No one comes to the Father except through Me" (John 14:6). How many other men have ever said that? Jesus even claimed that 1500 years before His birth, Moses wrote about Him and further, that the entire Old Testament bore witness to Him (John 6:46,47; Luke 24:27, 44).

Jesus commanded men to love Him in the exact same way that they love God—with all their heart, soul, and mind (Matthew 22:37,38). Jesus said that God the Holy Spirit would bear witness of Him and glorify Him (John 16:14). Who ever made such a claim? Jesus said that to know Him was to know God (John 14:7). To receive Him was to receive God (Matthew 10:40). To honor Him was to honor God (John 5:23). To believe in Him was to believe in God (John 12:44,45; 14:1). To see Him was to see God (John 8:19;14:7). To deny Him was to deny God (John 8:19, cf. 1 John 2:23). To hate Him was to hate God (John 15:23). Did any other religious founders in history ever make such statements?

In Mark 2, Jesus claimed He could forgive sins—something all religions concede is reserved for God alone. In John 10:28 and 11:25, He said He could give all who believed on Him eternal life. How can a mere man—indeed, anyone less than God—give eternal life to creatures who die? Yet Jesus raised the dead even in front of His enemies—not in some dark alley, but before scores of eyewitnesses (Luke 7:11-15; 8:41-42,49-56; John 11:43,44). Who ever did that? He did other miracles that amazed those who saw them:

"We have never seen anything like this!" (Mark 2:12).

"Nobody has ever heard of opening the eyes of a man born blind" (John 9:32).

In Matthew 25, He said that He would return at the end of the world and that He would judge every person who ever lived; He would personally raise all the dead of history and all the nations would be gathered before Him! Who else ever said that? He would sit on His throne of glory and judge and separate men from one another as a shepherd does the sheep from the goats (Matthew 25:31-46, cf. John 5:25-34). Just as clearly, Jesus taught that every person's eternal destiny depended upon how they treated Him (John 8:24; Matthew 10:32). All these statements, and many more like them, leave us little choice. Either Jesus was who He said He was—God incarnate—or else He was absolutely crazy. But who can believe *that*?

5. Why isn't Christianity intolerant or narrow-minded for teaching there is only one way to God?

We have seen that Jesus Christ stands alone when compared to the founders of other great religions. We have also mentioned that the creation parallels the nature of its Creator through its unity and diversity. So we could logically expect the same things for the Creator's approach to salvation. In other words, that salvation itself would stand alone and that, in ways, it would parallel the nature of the Creator and the nature of the creation.

Thus, first, Jesus is unique; Christian salvation is unique. Jesus is exclusively God's Son; salvation is exclusively through Jesus. Only Jesus died for sin; only Jesus can forgive sin. Only Jesus resurrected from the dead; only Jesus can resurrect others to eternal life.

Essentially, if there is only one true God, then there should be only one true way of salvation because the way of salvation must be consistent with the nature of the one true God—His grace, love, mercy, truth, etc. As Dr. Robert Morey comments, "Logically, since all religions contradict each other, there are only two options open to us. Either they are all false, or there is only *one* true religion. If there is only one God—there will be only *one* religion." If so, then isn't it possible that it is really the person who objects to this who is being narrow—too narrow to accept the truth?[63] The truth may be difficult but that is no reason to reject it.

Second, what we find to be true about God's creation is also true about the nature of salvation. Like everything else in the world, salvation must be done correctly to be successful. For example, consider some examples of how life works, or doesn't work:

What happens if you drive your car in reverse? Or stop in the middle of a busy freeway? What happens if you let your dog drive your car? Or if you drive on the wrong side of the road—or drive drunk?

The result of driving incorrectly is that you injure or kill yourself and others. Driving incorrectly sooner or later has consequences, even for the best driver in the world.

When you build a house, what happens if you place the glass where wood should be and wood where the glass should be? Or build in a flood zone? Or use highly flammable materials? The result is that your house is not functional, or you risk losing your home.

Consider playing tennis. What if you try to play tennis with a broken arm? Or use your hand as a racket? Or play with your side of the court under water? The result is you will lose the game.

Consider learning math or having surgery. What if you try to learn math by reading comic books? What if you're scheduled for a routine appendectomy and the surgeon takes out your brain instead? In either case, you're in trouble.

If everything in the world must be done correctly to be successful, and if our lives are literally filled with examples of the problems caused for us when we do things incorrectly, why should we conclude that salvation is any different? Why should we conclude there *won't* be consequences for doing salvation wrong?

Do we say it is being narrow-minded, intolerant or bigoted for us to drive sober or for surgeons to operate on us properly? Indeed, our very lives may be at stake. And if our lives are already at stake in worldly things, isn't it also possible that our souls may be at stake in spiritual things? But a life is only for a short period of time; a soul is forever.

Then how much more vital is it that we be certain that *salvation* be done correctly if our very *souls* are at stake? The point is that the Christian claim to exclusivity is *not* something that is out of harmony with how people experience life and with how the world functions. God made the world this way because He had to. Given His character, He also *had* to make the way of salvation through Christ and Christ alone. A fascinating, if detailed study of this can be found in the late Canadian Scholar Arthur C. Custance's *The Seed of the Woman* (1980).

Christianity is indeed exclusive—it claims that only those who believe in Christ will find salvation—but it is not narrow-minded, intolerant, or bigoted. *People* can be broad minded or narrow-minded but not *ideas*. *Ideas* are neither broad nor narrow—they are true or false. The claim that Christ is the only way of salvation is either true or false. This can be determined only on the basis of the evidence, which we briefly address below.

Those who think Christianity is intolerant should ask whether *other* religions and philosophies are really as tolerant as they *claim*. In fact, they usually aren't, as we documented elsewhere.[64] So why should only Christianity be singled out for criticism? Merely because Christianity is the most honest about its beliefs?

When people claim to be tolerant, open-minded, objective, and fair, one must question such claims based on biblical revelation. Biblically speaking, if people in their natural state, prior to regeneration, are said to be God's enemies (Romans 5:10) who deliberately *suppress* the truth by unrighteousness (Romans 1:18) and who, actually, hate God (Romans 1:30) where can we logically expect to find tolerance, neutrality, or objectivity regarding religion and philosophy?

Ironically, it is frequently those people who claim to be accepting and tolerant of almost anything who are not tolerant of one thing—Christian faith. Literally thousands of examples could be cited of bigotry, hypocrisy, narrow-mindedness, and intolerance expressed towards Christians for doing no more than living out the logical consequences of their own religious faith[65]—something that those who malign Christian faith often claim to defend in all religions. Indeed, we challenge our readers to find a single religion anywhere that accepts Christianity as being fully true. Obviously, there are none, because all religions claim *they* are fully true. Christianity *is* exclusive, but it is not intolerant. While it seeks to convert others to faith in Christ, it respects the right of all men to choose their own destinies. But if men's destinies are at stake in the issue of salvation, people everywhere should also rejoice that Christians are sharing the good news of the gospel of Jesus Christ. Because if Christianity really is true, Christians have no other choice.

6. Is the quality of evidence for the truth of Christianity compelling?

Christianity is unique in both the evidence upon which it rests and the doctrines it teaches. Dr. Robert A. Morey writes, "There is more than enough evidence on every hand from every department of human experience and knowledge to demonstrate that Christianity is true. . . . [It is] the faith of the non-Christian [that] is externally and internally groundless.

They are the ones who leap in the dark. Some, like Kierkegaard, have admitted this." Further, no one anywhere can deny that "Christianity stands unique and apart from all other religions by its doctrines."[66] Christianity is not just intellectually credible, whether considered philosophically, historically, scientifically, ethically, culturally, etc., but from an evidential perspective, actually superior to other world views, secular or religious.[67] If Christianity were obviously false, as some critics charge, how could such esteemed intellectuals as those quoted below logically make their declarations? Mortimer Adler is one of the world's leading philosophers. He is chairman of the board of editors for *The Encyclopedia Britannica*, architect of *The Great Books of the Western World* series and its phenomenal *Syntopicon*, director of the prestigious Institute for Philosophical Research in Chicago, and author of *Truth in Religion, Ten Philosophical Mistakes, How to Think About God*, and over twenty other challenging books. He asserts, "I believe Christianity is the only logical, consistent faith in the world."[68] How could Adler make such a statement? Because he knows it can't logically be made of any other religion.

Philosopher, historian, theologian, and trial attorney John Warwick Montgomery, who holds nine graduate degrees in various fields, argues, "The evidence for the truth of Christianity overwhelmingly outweighs competing religious claims and secular world views."[69] How could an individual of such intellectual caliber as Dr. Montgomery use a descriptive phrase such as "overwhelmingly outweighs" if it were obviously false? His 50 books and 100+ scholarly articles indicate exposure to a wide variety of non-Christian religious and secular philosophies.

Alvin Plantinga, widely considered to be the greatest Protestant philosopher, recalls, "For nearly my entire life I have been convinced of the truth of Christianity."[70] On what basis can one of the world's greatest philosophers make such a declaration if the evidence for Christianity is unconvincing?

Dr. Drew Trotter is executive director of the Center for Christian Studies at Charlottesville, Virginia. He holds a doctorate from Cambridge University. He argues that "logic and the evidence both point to the reality of absolute truth, and that truth is revealed in Christ."[71]

If we are looking for obvious truths, then perhaps we should consider the words of noted economist and sociologist, George F. Gilder, author of *Wealth and Poverty*, who asserts, "Christianity is true and its truth will be discovered anywhere you look very far."[72]

Such accolades could be multiplied repeatedly.[73] While testimonies per se mean little, if they are undergirded by the weight of evidence they can hardly be dismissed out of hand.

When one examines all the arguments and attacks made against Christianity for 2,000 years, by some of the greatest minds ever, guess what one finds? Not one is valid. And not one, individually or collectively, disproves Christianity. Even regarding the most difficult problems, such as the problem of evil, Christianity has the *best* answer of any religion or philosophy and the best solution to the problem. If the leading minds of the world have been unable to disprove Christianity, this may explain why many of the other leading minds in the world, including those from other religions, have accepted it. James Sire correctly points out in *Why Should Anyone Believe Anything At All?*, an argument for belief, religious or other, must be secured on the best evidence, validly argued, and able to refute the strongest objections that can be mustered against it.[74] In the area of finding God, only Christianity passes the test.

Obviously, if the God of the Bible has revealed Himself and if He is the only God—and if Christ is the only way of salvation—then we would expect convincing evidence in substantiation. Not just some evidence, or inferior evidence—so that a person has a dozen equally valid options in their choice of religion—but superior evidence. As Dr. John Warwick Montgomery asks:

> What if a revelational truth-claim did not turn on questions of theology and religious philosophy—on any kind of esoteric, fideistic method available only to those who are already "true believers"—but on the very reasoning employed in the law to determine questions of fact?. . . Eastern faiths and Islam, to take familiar examples, ask the uncommitted seeker to discover their truth experientially: the faith-experience will be self-validating. . . . Christianity, on the other hand, declares that the truth of its absolute claims rests squarely on certain historical facts, open to ordinary investigation. . . . The advantage of a jurisprudential approach lies in the difficulty of jettisoning it: legal standards of evidence developed as essential means of resolving the most intractable disputes in society. . . . Thus one cannot very well throw out legal reasoning merely because its application to Christianity results in a verdict for the Christian faith.[75]

If we assume that a God of truth is dedicated to truth and desires that men find Him, then what is the most logical place to begin our search for the one true religion? And is there a religion that God has made stand apart from all others? Logically, the best, and only practical, way to see if one religion is absolutely true is to start with the largest, most unique, influential, and evidentiary religion in the world. It is much more reasonable to determine whether or not *this* religion is true than to seek another approach to the issue such as examining, one by one, all religions from A to Z, or picking one randomly or by personal preference.

All non-Christian religions are experientially based. As such, they cannot be proven because of their inherent subjectivism. So having profound religious experiences alone cannot prove such a religion is true. And, obviously, to attempt to examine *all* religions (whether the sequence is random, preferential, or alphabetical) would be a daunting and confusing, if not impossible, task. Regardless, if there is only one God and if only one religion is fully true, then one should not expect to discover sustainable evidence in any other religion. And indeed, no other religion, anywhere, large or small, has sustainable evidence in its favor. If no credible evidence exists for any other religion and only Christianity has compelling evidence, why should any time at all be spent examining religions that have no basis to substantiate their claims? Especially if there may be significant consequences for trusting in false religion, both in this life and the next?

It is much easier, and much more logical, to start by examining probabilities of truth on the highest end of the scale. In "The Value of an Evidential Approach," William J. Cairney (Ph.D., Cornell) discusses some of the possibilities that constitute genuine evidence for the fact God has inspired the Bible and the Christianity based on it:

> *History Written in Advance.* We can all write history in retrospect, but an almighty, omnipotent Creator would not be bound by our notions of space and time, and would thus be able to write history before it occurs. Suppose that we encountered a sourcebook that contained page after page of history written in advance with such accuracy and in such detail that good guessing would be completely ruled out.

> *Prescience.* Suppose that in this same sourcebook, we were able to find accurate statements written ages ago demonstrating scientific knowledge and concepts far

before mankind had developed the technological base necessary for discovering that knowledge or those concepts. . . .

Historical Evidence. Suppose that in this same sourcebook, we were to find historical assertions that time after time were verified as true as historical scholarship continued. . . .

Archaeological Evidence. Suppose that in this same sourcebook, statements that are difficult to verify are made about people and places, but as archaeology "unearths" more knowledge of the past, time after time the sourcebook is seen to be true in its assertions.

Philosophical and Logical Coherence. Suppose that this same sourcebook, even though written piecemeal over thousands of years, contains well-developed common themes and is internally consistent.

And suppose all of these evidences hang together without internal contradiction or literary stress within the same anthology. Collectively, we could not take these evidences lightly.[76]

Overall, the evidence strongly asserts that Christianity *is* true, whether that evidence is internal (the documents), philosophical, moral, historical, scientific, archaeological, or when compared with the evidence found in other religions. For example, "The competence of the New Testament documents would be established in any court of law" and "Modern archaeological research has confirmed again and again the reliability of New Testament geography, chronology, and general history."[77] Further, as the noted classical scholar Professor E. M. Blaiklock points out, "Recent archaeology has destroyed much nonsense and will destroy more. And I use the word nonsense deliberately, for theories and speculations find currency in [liberal] biblical scholarship that would not be tolerated for a moment in any other branch of literary or historical criticism."[78]

In essence, only Christianity meets the burden of proof necessary to say "This religion alone is fully true." That means Jesus Christ really is the only way of salvation. And no one can argue successfully that Christianity has not been thoroughly investigated: As the fifth edition of *Man's Religions* by John B. Noss points out, "The first Christian century has had more books written about it than any other

38

comparable period of history. The chief sources bearing on its history are the gospels and epistles of the New Testament, and these—again we must make a comparative statement— have been more thoroughly searched by inquiring minds than any other books ever written."[79]

7. What are some specific examples of the evidence for Christianity?

Among many possible lines of evidence for Christianity, we have selected two we feel will command the attention of any open-minded person—specifically, fufilled prophecy and the historical resurrection of Jesus Christ. First, the existence of specifically fulfilled prophecy in the Bible cannot be denied. For example, the internal and external evidence both clearly support a pre-neo-Babylonian composition for the book of Isaiah (seventh century BC) and a neo-Babylonian composition for the book of Daniel (sixth century BC).[80] Yet Isaiah predicts and describes what King Cyrus will do (by name) over 100 years before he even lived (Isaiah 44:28–45:6). Isaiah also describes the specific nature and death of the Jewish Messiah 700 years in advance (Isaiah 9:6; 53:1-12), and the Babylonian captivity of Judah 100 years in advance (Isaiah 39:5-7). Indeed, the Assyrian captivity is hinted at by Moses as early as 1400 BC in Deuteronomy 28:64-66.

Similarly, in 530 BC, hundreds of years in advance, the prophet Daniel (Matthew 24:15) predicts the Medo-Persian, Greek, and Roman empires so clearly that antisupernatural- ists are forced, against all the evidence, to date this book at 165 BC and thus imply it is a forgery (cf., Daniel 2, 7, 11:1-35 in light of subsequent Persian, Greek, and Roman history and the dynasties of the Egyptians and Syrians).[81] I Kings 13:1,2 predicts King Josiah 300 years before he was born, and Micah 5:2 predicts the very birthplace of Jesus 700 years before He was born. In *Knowing the Truth About Jesus the Messiah*, we provided a great deal of additional evidence of supernatural prophecy in the Bible, and we show why this is impossible to explain apart from the divine inspiration of the Bible. How are we to account for such things if the Bible is not a book inspired by God? Nothing like this is found in other religions.

Second, nothing like the historical resurrection of Christ is found in other religions. As *Newsweek* magazine commented in its cover story for April 8, 1996 (p. 61), "By any measure the resurrection of Jesus is the most radical of Christian doc trines. . . . of no other historical figure has the claim been made persistently that God has raised him from the dead."

In light of the evidence, the resurrection cannot logically be denied and, if it is true, given the teachings of Jesus, it proves beyond a reasonable doubt that Christianity alone is fully true. (See our *Knowing the Truth about the Resurrection.*)

How? On the authority of accepted principles of historic and textual analysis, the New Testament documents can be shown to be reliable and trustworthy. That is, they give accurate primary source evidence for the life and death of Jesus Christ. In 2,000 years the New Testament authors have never been proven unethical, dishonest, or the object of deception. In the Gospel records, Jesus claims to be God incarnate (John 5:18;10:27-33); He exercises innumerable divine prerogatives, and fully rests His claims on His numerous, abundantly testified, historically unparalleled miracles (John 10:37,38), and His forthcoming physical resurrection from the dead (John 10:17,18). No one else ever did this.

Christ's resurrection is minutely described in the gospels; it was subject to repeated eyewitness verification by skeptics; and over 2,000 years it has never been disproved despite the detailed scholarship of the world's best skeptics. Nor can the resurrection be rejected *a priori* on antisupernaturalist grounds, for miracles are impossible only if so defined. The probability of a miracle is determined by the cumulative weight of the evidence, not philosophical bias.

To illustrate the quality of the evidence for the resurrection, a two-day public debate was held between Dr. Gary R. Habermas, a Christian scholar, and Anthony Flew, a leading philosopher and skeptic of the resurrection. Ten independent judges, all of whom served on the faculty of American universities, were to render a verdict. The first panel of judges was composed of five philosophers who were instructed to evaluate the debate content and judge the winner. The second panel of judges were told to evaluate the argumentation technique of the debaters.

The results on content were four votes in favor of the Christian argument, one vote for a draw, and no vote in favor of the skeptical position. The decision on argumentation technique was three to two in favor of the Christian debater. The overall decision of both panels was seven to two in favor of the Christian position, with one draw. With one of the world's leading philosophers defending the skeptical position, the judges were often surprised that the outcome resulted so heavily in favor of the resurrection. The details are given in *Did Jesus Rise From the Dead? The Resurrection Debate* (Terry L. Miethe, ed., Harper & Row, 1987). But the fact is that hundreds of such professional debates on the resurrection,

the existence of God, the creation-evolution controversy, etc.,
have now been held. And Christians characteristically win
the debates. If Christian truth claims withstand all counter
arguments and win in scholarly debate, isn't this compelling
evidence Christianity is true?

8. Why is the resurrection important to each of us personally?

In *The Son Rises*, an excellent text on the historical and logical evidence for the resurrection, Dr. William Lane Craig
gives the following important anecdote:

> "There ain't gonna be no Easter this year," a student
> friend remarked to me.
>
> "Why not?" I asked incredulously.
>
> "They found the body."
>
> Despite his irreverent humor, my friend displayed a
> measure of insight often not shared by modern [liberal]
> theologians. His joke correctly perceived that without the
> resurrection Christianity is worthless.
>
> The earliest Christians would certainly have agreed
> with my friend. The apostle Paul put it straight and
> simple: "If Christ was not raised then neither our
> preaching nor your faith has any meaning at all. . . . If
> Christ did not rise your faith is futile and your sins
> have never been forgiven" (1 Corinthians 15:14,17,
> PHILLIPS). For the earliest Christians, Jesus' resurrection
> was a historical fact, every bit as real as His death on
> the cross. Without the resurrection, Christianity would
> have been simply false. Jesus would have been just
> another prophet who had met His unfortunate fate at
> the hands of the Jews. Faith in Him as Lord, Messiah,
> or Son of God would have been stupid. There would
> be no use in trying to save the situation by interpreting
> the resurrection as some sort of symbol. The cold, hard
> facts of reality would remain: Jesus was dead and any-
> thing He started died with Him.
>
> David C. K. Watson tells the true story of another man
> who understood this, with tragic consequences. The man
> was a retired clergyman who in his spare time began to
> study the thought of certain modern theologians on the
> resurrection. He read books on the resurrection and

watched television talk shows on the subject. In his old age, he felt sure that the highly educated professors and writers knew far more than he did and that they were surely right when they said Jesus had not literally risen from the dead. He understood clearly what that meant for him: His whole life and ministry had been based on a bundle of lies. He committed suicide.

I believe that modern theologians must answer to God for that man's death. One cannot make statements on such matters without accepting part of the responsibility for the consequences. The average layman probably expects that theologians would be biased in favor of the resurrection, when in fact exactly the opposite is often true. It has not been historians who have denied the historical resurrection of Jesus, but theologians. Why this strange situation? According to Carl Braaten, theologians who deny the resurrection have not done so on historical grounds; rather theology has been derailed by existentialism and historicism, which have a stranglehold on the formation of theological statements. Hence, the statements of many theologians concerning the resurrection of Jesus actually are not based on fact, but are determined by philosophical assumptions. That makes statements that deny that Jesus' resurrection was a historical fact all the more irresponsible, for their conclusion has not been determined by the facts, which support the historicity of the resurrection, but by assumptions.

The point is that the Christian faith stands or falls with the resurrection of Jesus. It is no use saying, as some theologians do, "We believe in the risen Christ, not in the empty tomb!". . . If Jesus did not rise from the dead, then He was a tragedy and a failure, and no amount of theologizing or symbolizing could change the situation.[82]

Christianity is the only religion on earth which stands or falls on the truthfulness of a single event in history, an event that happened 2,000 years ago.

Christianity has stood the test of time.

Dr. Craig concludes with the following comments:

1. "The resurrection of Jesus was an act of God. . . . Anyone who denies this explanation is rationally obligated to produce a more plausible cause of Jesus' resurrection and to explain how it happened. . . .

2. The resurrection of Jesus confirms His personal claims. . . .

3. The resurrection of Jesus shows that He holds the key to eternal life."[83]

If Jesus rose from the dead, something no one else has done, this strongly validates His claims to be God incarnate. If so, Jesus is an infallible authority—and it was Jesus Himself who taught He was the only way to God (John 14:6). If no one else in history ever rose from the dead, on what *logical* basis can the claims of Jesus be doubted? The value of the resurrection for us personally is that, if we believe in Jesus, it supplies *proof* of our forgiveness before God and full assurance of our final salvation, that we will go to heaven when we die. (Please see Romans 4:25; John 3:16;5:24;6:37; Romans 8:28-39; 1 John 5:13.) No such assurance of salvation exists in any other religion on earth.

Everyone must die. The Bible teaches that everyone must also live forever—the only question is where they will live. Our conclusion is that the miraculous nature of the Bible, which speaks for its divine inspiration, as well as Christ's own resurrection and His infallible pronouncements as God incarnate concerning the true way of salvation are more than sufficient reason to accept the Christian view that all men and women will spend eternity in either a place called heaven or a place called hell.

In light of our discussion to date, please consider what the inspired Word of God and Jesus Christ, the incarnate Son of God, taught about salvation. Again, Christianity makes claims about the uniqueness, originality and exclusiveness of its God and Founder that no other religion makes:

Exodus 20:2,3—I am the Lord your God ... you shall have no other gods before me.

Isaiah 43:10,11 (NASB)—Before Me there was no God formed, and there will be none after Me. I, even I, am the Lord; and there is no savior besides Me.

John 14:6 (NASB) —I am the way, and the truth, and the life; no one comes to the Father, but through Me.

John 17:3 (NASB)—And this is eternal life, that they may know Thee, the only true God, and Jesus Christ whom Thou hast sent.

Acts 4:12 (NASB)—And there is salvation in no one else; for there is no other name under heaven that has been given among men, by which we must be saved.

1 Timothy 2:5-6 (NASB)—For there is one God, and one mediator also between God and men, the man Christ Jesus, who gave Himself as a ransom for all, the testimony borne at the proper time.

Jesus is unique in His love, holiness, authority, majesty, humility, and impact in the world. Among all the religious leaders and founders, past or present, He alone was sinless. And to be without sin means to be incapable of telling a lie and always telling the truth. Therefore, when He said, "For God so loved the world that he gave his one and only Son, that whoever believes in him shall not perish but have eternal life" (John 3:16), He was speaking the truth.

If you desire to live forever in heaven with Jesus Christ, the only true Savior, we would encourage you to pray the following prayer:

> Lord Jesus Christ, I humbly acknowledge that I have sinned in my thinking, speaking and acting, that I am guilty of deliberate wrongdoing, that my sins have separated me from Your holy presence, and that I am helpless to commend myself to You.

> I firmly believe that You died on the cross for my sins, bearing them in Your own body and suffering in my place the condemnation they deserved.

> I have thoughtfully counted the cost of following You. I sincerely repent, turning away from my past sins. I am willing to surrender to You as my Lord and Master. Help me not to be ashamed of You.

> So now I come to You. I believe that for a long time You have been patiently standing outside the door knocking. I now open the door. Come in, Lord Jesus, and be my Savior and my Lord forever. Amen.[84]

He is there, He hears, and He answers.

If you have prayed this prayer we encourage you to write us directly at The John Ankerberg Show. We want to help your growth as a Christian. Next, we suggest that you read a modern, easy to read translation of the Bible such as the New International Version or New American Standard Bible. Start with the New Testament, Psalms and Proverbs and then proceed to the rest of the Scriptures. Also, find a quality church where people honor the Bible and God's Word and Jesus Christ as their personal Lord and Savior. Tell someone of your decision to follow Christ and begin to grow in your new relationship with God by talking to Him daily in prayer.

Notes

1. In *Religious and Theological Studies Fellowship Bulletin*, Nov./Dec., 1994, p. 22.

2. Douglas Groothuis, "When the Salt Loses Its Savor," *CRI Journal*, Winter, 1995, p. 50.

3. Mortimer J. Adler, "A Philosopher's Religious Faith," in Kelly James Clark (ed.), *Philosophers Who Believe: The Spiritual Journeys of Eleven Leading Thinkers* (Downer's Grove, IL: InterVarsity, 1993), p. 207.

4. G. K. Chesterton, *The Everlasting Man* (Garden City, NY: Image, 1985), p. 19.

5. Maureen OHara, "Science, Pseudo-Science, and Myth Mongering," in Robert Basil (ed.), *Not Necessarily the New Age: Critical Essays* (NY: Prometheus, 1988), p. 148.

6. William Lane Craig, *Reasonable Faith: Christian Truth and Apologetics* (Wheaton, IL: Crossway Books, 1994), pp. xiii-xv.

7. See our book, *The Facts On Creation Vs. Evolution* (Eugene, OR: Harvest House, 1994) and our forthcoming book-length treatment.

8. This statement does not hold true where Roman Catholic beliefs are biblical. Nevertheless, the evidence upon which official, traditional Roman Catholic dogma and related practice rests is unconvincing.

9. For a critique of naturalism see Phillip E. Johnson, *Reason in the Balance: The Case Against NATURALISM in Science, Law & Education* (Downer's Grove, IL: InterVarsity, 1995).

10. Isaac Newton, *Mathematical Principles of Natural Philosophy*, trans. Andrew Motte (1714; rev. and ed., Florian Cajori, Berkeley, CA: University of California, 1934), p. 32.

11. See, e.g., Henry Morris, *Men of Science, Men of Faith* (Santee, CA: Creation-Life, 1990). See note 9.

12. E.g., Roy Abraham Varghese, *The Intellectuals Speak Out About God* (Dallas: Lewis & Stanley, 1984); Kelly James Clark (ed.), *Philosophers Who Believe: The Spiritual Journeys of Eleven Leading Thinkers* (Downer's Grove, IL: InterVarsity, 1993); Henry Margenau and Roy Abraham Varghese, eds., *Cosmos, Bios, Theos: Scientists Reflect on Science, God and the Origin of the Universe, Life and Homo Sapiens* (LaSalle, IL: Open Court, 1992).

13. Terrance A. Sweeney, *God And* (Minneapolis, MN: Winston Press, 1985).

14. Carl Jung (H.G. and C.F. Baynes, translators), *Two Essays in Analytical Psychology* (NY: Dodd Mead, 1928), p. 73, cited in Rollo May, *The Art of Counseling* (NY: Abingdon, 1967), p. 217.

15. Interview by Doug Wead, "George Bush: Where Does He Stand?," *Christian Herald*, June 1986, p. 14.

16. Whenever there are problems or tragedies in life and God does not seem to be "kind and good," so to speak when we see famines or crime or evil governments or natural disasters, we should never doubt God's goodness. (See John Wenham, *The Goodness of God*; C. S. Lewis, *The Problem of Pain*.) These things result from a fallen natural order, our sin, the devil, or the folly of men, not from God, e.g., the greed and stupidity of men cause calamities such as famines in communist and socialist regimes, and the evil done by dictators and drug runners destroys thousands or millions of lives. Sometimes evil reaches such proportions that God *is* forced by His own righteousness to send judgment in various forms through weather calamities, economic hardships, etc. Of course, natural and social disasters are not always the direct judgment of God, but if God did not uphold His own holiness and punish evil, things would be far worse than they are. As it is, God is much more merciful and longsuffering than we deserve and far

more merciful and longsuffering to evil men than most of us would be. Further, the Bible tells us that all men intuitively know God is good despite the evil in the world (Romans 1:18-21;2:14-16;3:4-6). If God were *truly* evil, there would be no hope and the conditions of life and our sense of things would be quite different. This is why we never ask, "Why is there so much good in the world?" but instead we ask, "Why is there so much evil in the world?" We know that evil is the aberration in a universe whose ruler is good and righteous. And in fact, the evil that exists is not as prevalent as suggested by our instantaneous, worldwide media reporting and, again, it could be much worse were it not for God's restraining hand (2 Thessalonians 2:6,7) and His common grace. On the other hand, things generally are much worse than they need to be because our culture rejects moral absolutes and our children are raised in an environment of relativism that can justify almost any behavior.

17. Quotations from the 1987 Rainbow calendar, (Allen, TX: Argus Communications), Product #14850.

18. Lewis Thomas, *The Medusa and the Snail*, (NY: Viking Press, 1979), pp. 155-157.

19. Taoist priest and scholar Kenneth Cohen, "Chi, the Breath of Life," *Yoga Journal*, March/April, 1986, p. 37.

20. Adler, in Clark (ed.), *Philosophers Who Believe*, p. 209, emphasis added.

21. Examining the context in which this quotation occurs is instructive. Huxley was frank enough to confess that his desire to be free from the Christian God and morality was based more upon emotional considerations than rational ones: "For myself, as, no doubt, for most of my contemporaries, the philosophy of meaninglessness was essentially an instrument of liberation. The liberation we desired was simultaneously liberation from a certain political and economic system and liberation from a certain system of morality. We objected to the morality because it interfered with our sexual freedom; we objected to the political and economic system because it was unjust. The supporters of these systems claimed that in some way they embodied the meaning (a Christian meaning, they insisted) of the world. There was one admirably simple method of confuting these people and at the same time justifying ourselves in our political and erotic revolt: We could deny that the world had any meaning whatsoever." As Huxley wrote further, "I had motives for not wanting the world to have a meaning; consequently I assumed that it had none, and was able without any difficulty to find satisfying reasons for this assumption. Most ignorance is vincible ignorance. We don't know because we don't want to know. It is our will that decides how and upon which subjects we shall use our intelligence. Those who detect no meaning in the world generally do so because, for one reason or another, it suits their books that the world should be meaningless."[22] But as Ravi Zacharias points out, the atrocities committed historically that are the logical consequences of the antitheistic position are far deeper and more severe than for those (inconsistently) committed in the name of Christianity: "Conveniently forgotten by those antagonistic to spiritual issues are the far more devastating consequences that have entailed when antitheism is wedded to political theory and social engineering. There is nothing in history to match the dire ends to which humanity can be led by following a political and social philosophy that consciously and absolutely excludes God." And, "One of the great blind spots of a philosophy that attempts to disavow God is its unwillingness to look into the face of the monster it has begotten and own up to being its creator." Indeed, "The infrastructure of our society has become mindless and senseless because the foundation upon which we have built cannot support any other kind of structure." (Ravi Zacharias, *Can Man Live Without God?* (Dallas: Word, 1994), XVII, 21, 22).

22. Aldous Huxley, *Ends and Means*, (London: Chatto & Windus, 1946), pp. 270, 273, emphasis added.

23. Sir John Eccles and Daniel N. Robinson, *The Wonder of Being Human: Our Brain and Our Mind* (Boston: Shambhala/New Science Library, 1985), pp. 178-179.

24. In Robert Kastenbaum, *Is There Life After Death?* (NY: Prentice Hall, 1984), p. 9 citing Bertrand Russell, *The Autobiography of Bertrand Russell*, Vol. 2 (Boston: Little Brown & Co.), 1968, pp. 95-96.

25. Aniela Jaffe (ed.), *C. G. Jung Memories, Dreams, Reflections* (NY: Vintage, 1965), p. xi.

26. Ibid.

27. William Warren Bartley, III, *Werner Erhard: The Transformation of a Man: The Founding of est* (NY: Clarkson & Potter, Inc., 1978), p. 92.

28. *Seikyo Times*, October, 1982, p. 55.

29. Jean Bolen, *The Tao of Psychology* (San Francisco: Harper & Row, 1982), p. 7.

30. Ibid., p. 2, last emphasis added.

31. Ibid., p. 1.

32. Editorial, *Reader's Digest*, August, 1987, p. 117.

33. Simone de Beauvoir, "A Conversation About Death and God," *Harper's* magazine, February, 1984, p. 39.

34. Ibid., p 38.

35. Ibid., p. 39, emphasis added

36. Clark H. Pinnock, "Cultural Apologetics: An Evangelical Standpoint," *Bibliotheca Sacra*, January-March, 1970, p. 61, citing Charles L. Glicksberg, *Literature and Religion*, p. 221.

37. Haim Gordon, "Sartre's Struggle Against the Holy," *International Journal for Philosophy of Religion* (NY: Abingdon, 1967), Vol. 19 (1986), p. 95.

38. Don Richardson, *Eternity in Their Hearts* (Ventura, CA: Regal Books, 1981), pp. 53-54.

39. Rollo May, *The Art of Counseling* (NY: Abingdon, 1967), p. 215.

40. Cited in *Los Angeles Times*, June 28, 1986. We could not confirm this research. Convinced philosophical atheists clearly could pass lie detector tests since these measure conviction of belief. But such results, if valid, show that many practical, as opposed to philosophical, atheists really aren't so sure of their views.

41. Sweeney, p. 203.

42. Cited in Clark Pinnock, *Set Forth Your Case* (Chicago: Moody Press, 1971), p. 9.

43. Jean-Paul Sartre, *Being and Nothingness* (London: Methuen, 1957), p. 566.

44. Frits Staal, "Indian Concepts of the Body," *Somatics*, Autumn/Winter 1983-1984, p. 33.

45. Ajith Fernando, *The Supremacy of Christ* (Wheaton, IL: Crossway, 1995), p. 241.

46. Leslie Paul, *The Annihilation of Man* (NY: Harcourt Brace, 1945), p. 154, from Arthur Custance, *A Framework of History* (Doorway Paper, #29 Ottawa, 1968), p. III.

47. Albert Camus, *The Rebel*, A. Bower, trans. (Harmondsworth: Penguin, 1962), p. 16, from Os Guiness, *The Dust of Death* (Downer's Grove, IL: InterVarsity, 1973), p. 37.

48. Cited in Clark Pinnock, *Live Now Brother* (Chicago: Moody Press, 1972), p. 18.

49. Walter Kaufman, *Nietzsche* (NY: Vintage, 1968), p. 97, citing *Nietzsche, The Gay Science* (1882), p. 125. The full citation is given in Frederick Nietzesche, "The Madman," a section of *The Gay Science* in Walter Kaufman, ed., *The Portable Nietzesche* (NY: Viking, 1954), p. 125.

50. Kaufman, *Nietzsche*, p. 97.

51. Scholarly works such as W. R. Bird's *The Origin of Species Revisited* (Philosophical Library, 2 Vols., 1993), Michael Denton's *Evolution: A Theory in Crisis* (Adler & Adler, 1986), A. E. Wilder-Smith's *The Natural Sciences Know Nothing of Evolution* (Master Books, 1981), Phillip E. Johnson's *Darwin on Trial* (InterVarsity, 1993), James Coppedge's *Evolution: Possible Or Impossible?* (Zondervan, 1973), and many others should prove this to any thinking person who does not allow naturalistic philosophical biases to dominate his world view. In addition, books like J. P. Moreland's (ed.) *The Creation Hypothesis: Scientific Evidence for An Intelligent Designer* (Inter-Varsity, 1994)

and A. E. Wilder-Smith's *The Scientific Alternative to Neo- Darwinian Evolutionary Theory* (T.W.F.P. Publishers, 1987) demonstrate that there is solid scientific evidence for a rational belief in creationism. Books such as Robert Clarke's and James Bales' *Why Scientists Accept Evolution* (Baker, 1976) and Phillip E. Johnson's *Reason in the Balance: The Case Against NATURALISM in Science, Law and Education* (InterVarsity, 1995) provide additional important information on this issue. In general, the academic qualifications of the authors of these books are both highly distinguished and impeccable.

52. Sura 3:138, "The House of Inram," A. J. Arberry, Trans., *The Koran Interpreted* (NY: Macmillan, 1976), p. 91; Sura, "The Night Journey," in N. J. Dawood, trans., *The Koran*, (Baltimore, MD: Penguin, 1972), p. 235.

53. *The Koran*, J. M. Rodwell, Trans. (NY: Dutton), pp. 244, 384, 423, 460, 468, etc. (Sura 4:106; 40:57; 47:21; 48:2; 110:3).

54. Robert O. Ballou, *The Portable World Bible: A Comprehensive Selection from the Eight Great Sacred Scriptures of the World* (NY: The Viking Press, 1968), pp. 134, 147, 151.

55. Houston Smith, *The Religions of Man* (NY: Harper & Row, 1965), p. 99.

56. Clive Erricker, *Buddhism*, (Chicago: NTC Publishing, 1995), pp. 2,3.

57. Arthur Waley, trans., *The Analects of Confucius* (NY: Vintage, 1938), p. 130.

58. Yasna, 44:11; Moulton, Ez.368; from Robert E. Hume, *The World's Living Religions* (NY: Charles Scribner's Sons, 1959), rev., p. 203.

59. *Tao-The-King*, 20:3, 20:5-7 cited in Hume, p. 136.

60. Hume, p. 95.

61. Ibid., p. 283.

62. Ibid., pp. 285-286.

63. Robert A. Morey, *Introduction to Defending the Faith* (Southbridge, MA: Crowne Publications, 1989), p. 38.

64 The longer version of this booklet, on file at Ankerberg Theological Research Institute.

65. For illustrations in science see Jerry Bergman, *The Criterion* (Richfield, MN: Onesimus, 1984).

66. Morey, pp. 9-10, 43.

67. Dr. Weldon is currently working piecemeal on a lengthy volume on this subject. It will become volume five or six in the Harvest House encyclopedia series, or be published separately.

68. As cited in an interview in *Christianity Today*, November 19, 1990, p. 34.

69. John W. Montgomery (ed.), *Evidence for Faith: Deciding the God Question* (Dallas: Word, 1991), p. 9.

70. Alvin Plantinga, "A Christian Life Partly Lived," in Kelly James-Clark (ed.), *Philosophers Who Believe* (Downer's Grove, IL: InterVarsity, 1993), p. 69.

71. As interviewed in the *Chattanooga Free Press*, July 23, 1995, p. A-11.

72. L. Neff, "Christianity Today Talks to George Gilder," *Christianity Today*, March 6, 1987, p. 35, cited in David A. Noebel, *Understanding the Times: The Religious Worldviews of Our Day and the Search for Truth* (Eugene, OR: Harvest House, 1994), p. 13.

73. For testimony of skeptics' conversion to Christianity based on the evidence for the resurrection of Christ, see *Do the Resurrection Accounts Conflict? and What Proof Is There That Jesus Rose From the Dead?* (Chattanooga, TN: The John Ankerberg Theological Research Institute, 1990), to be republished in a revised and expanded edition by Harvest House Publishers, 1997, or see the articles in *The Ankerberg Theological Research Institute News Magazine*, Vol. 2, no. 3, March 1995, and Vol. 2, no. 4, April 1995.

74. James Sire, *Why Should Anyone Believe Anything At All?* (Downer's Grove, IL: InterVarsity Press, 1994), p. 10.

75. John Warwick Montgomery, "The Jury Returns: A Juridical Defense of Christianity," in John Warwick Montgomery (ed.), *Evidence for Faith: Deciding the God Question* (Dallas: Word/Probe Books, 1991), pp. 319-320.

76. William J. Cairney, "The Value of an Evidential Approach," in Montgomery (ed.), *Evidence for Faith*, p. 21.

77. Montgomery, "The Jury Returns: A Juridical Defense of Christianity," in Montgomery (ed.), *Evidence for Faith*, pp. 322, 326.
78. E. M. Blaiklock, *Christianity Today*, Sept. 28, 1973, p. 13.
79. John B. Noss, *Man's Religions*, 5th ed., (NY: Macmillan, 1974), p. 417.
80. Bruce K. Waltke, "The Date of the Book of Daniel," in Roy B. Zuck (gen. ed.), *Vital Apologetic Issues: Examining Reason and Revelation in Biblical Perspective* (Grand Rapids, MI: Kregel, 1995), pp. 194-203; for Daniel and Isaiah see Gleason L. Archer, Jr., *A Survey of Old Testament Introduction* (Chicago: Moody Press, Rev. 1974).
81. See the commentaries on Daniel by John F. Walvoord, Charles Lee Feinberg, and H. C. Lenpold.
82. William Lane Craig, *The Son Rises* (Chicago: Moody Press, 1981), pp. 135-136.
83. Ibid., 136.
84. Taken from John Stott, *Becoming a Christian* (Downer's Grove, IL: InterVarsity, 1950), p. 25-26.